THE LAST SONG

Aaron Kent is a working-class writer and insomniac from Cornwall. His work has been praised by the likes of JH Prynne, Gillian Clarke, Andre Bagoo, Andrew McMillan, and Anthony (Vahni) Capildeo. Aaron was awarded the Awen medal from the Bards of Cornwall in 2020, then subsequently suffered a brain haemorrhage a few months later. Coincidence? Probably.

Maria Sledmere is a lecturer and lapsed music journalist based in Glasgow. She is editor-in-chief of SPAM Press and author of poetry books including Visions & Feed (HVTN Press, 2022), String Feeling (Erotoplasty Editions, 2022) and The Luna Erratum (Dostoyevsky Wannabe, 2021). The latter was shortlisted for the Saltire Society's Scottish Poetry Book of the Year 2022.

Anthologies from Broken Sleep Books

Contents

ISBN: 978-1-915760-92-0

Cover designed by Aaron Kent

Edited and typeset by Aaron Kent

Broken Sleep Books Ltd   Broken Sleep Books Ltd
Rhydwen   Fair View
Talgarreg   Nanpean
Ceredigion   Cornwall
SA44 4HB   PL26 7YH

The Last Song:
Words for Frightened Rabbit

Edited by Aaron Kent & Maria Sledmere

Foreword

Where now, the Frightened Rabbit? In Emma Whitelaw's 'It's got lots to do with magnets and the pull of the moon', our speaker translates from 'rabblish' that 'long for the cold' which is a rabbit heart, pleading for the moon, 'a very old soul'. If you grow up in Scotland, you get to know that call of the moon on a long winter's night, breath making special effects of the freezing air, the hot drunken shriek of your pals around you. It might be that Frightened Rabbit are a band for old souls, those who saw before their time something magnificent or terrible flashing in the headlights. If you've heard a wall of guitars, a voice croon of woah-oh-oh-oh-ohhhh, a drumroll like a wrestle, maybe you've felt the same.

What is it to be struck by fear? The poems in this anthology offer shelters, inlets, points of departure, beams of light, pools of shade. 'Let's hide here a while', implores Andrew Blair's speaker in 'Ramshackle'. When we announced the call for submissions, Aaron and I were looking for poems which might crack open the lyric form to reveal the fissures where the music of Frightened Rabbit had weathered in. The works selected draw inspiration from the band's sonic landscapes and emotional gales, like a folk music of the grieving, not sufficiently in sync to form a chorus. Those who chose the pull of the sea, its chaos. Who find their own tides in the afterglow.

'I'm singing the greys for you while the sea bleeds', writes Lynn Valentine in 'Crawling'. Water runs through many of these poems, a metaphor and more, 'Grief is the sea lappin' / it ma feet' (M McCorquodale, 'Glasgae Blessin'). Shorn up together, that flow begins to crystallise and fall, softly to words. The first time I went to see Frightened Rabbit, I could not go because of cancelled trains and a heavy snow. I was just a teenager with chilblains, forlorn at the station. Years later, in my beloved music journalism era, I saw Scott Hutchison playing solo in a friend's flat, generously appeasing our host's pleas to play 'It's Christmas so We'll Stop'. Whisky-warm and the spell of it, December 2017. There's a home video quality to many of these poems: VHS flickers of something half-remembered, 'skys – always plurals' (Michelle Moloney), 'Sunbeams and a face / like the middle of a flower' (Jade King). What does poetry offer but a social charm, a state of suspension, transformation, red-eyed and pedalling; here where the rot stops, press pause.

While reading these poems, look for tiny acts, threads and miracles between the lines. Have a lost weekend with us. This is a collection of resonance, the greys between, the contingent form of what it means to be 'still swimming' (Valentine). I see a Frightened Rabbit in every 'I'. A special trembling, a bright exposure; the 'snowball traction' (Julian Colton) of an intimacy which hits across the sea, an elegy belonging to everyone.

— *Maria Sledmere*

* * *

When I first started writing poetry, I spoke to a famous American hip-hop artist about creativity, about why we write, and he drew attention to something I had put in a bio on social media, *while I'm alive, I'll make tiny changes to Earth.* He asked why I only wanted to make tiny changes, why would I aim so low?

The tiny changes we make could be a burst of motivation somebody gets from reading a line of poetry or listening to a three minute track. Those tiny changes could be learning to pronounce somebody's name correctly, or offering space to somebody who didn't think they warranted it. Tiny changes are the things that we leave behind without selfishness, without the myopic lens of self-improvement — they're the things we receive without realising we've done so.

Frightened Rabbit were a band of tiny changes, of such delicate impact that it would be difficult to quantify the good they did. Every contribution to this anthology is another grain of sand in the beach left behind, another minute seashell carved by their work.

Sometimes the tiny changes matter as much as the big ones, sometimes a small difference is the biggest difference. Scott, Grant, Billy, Andy, Simon, and Gordon weren't afraid to make music that made a change, and this anthology is testament to that.

— *Aaron Kent*

homeless wind

come gather in my lungs homeless wind
hush your blackest poems
as the ships around us sink
and then idle in my lungs cold homeless wind

come rest upon my shoulders homeless rain
the late buds of this month will likely never come again
but you don't have to drum out this entire sad refrain
come sleep upon my shoulders homeless rain

we can take the stupid cosmos it's ok
I'll flex my wrists against the terror
push it miles and miles away
don't thank me listen really it's ok

A Song Not Sung.

1.

With the tide, the deep and low comes, sits inside, is dark and slow
the waves that wash through generations by the river's mouth
where its harbours let us settle by the Forth to work
in shipyards, gutting fish or taking ships to sea
a woman from my mother's side once saved a man from drowning at Queensferry
near the bridges; in the photograph we have of her, in our front room,
the pupils of her eyes look painted, deep and dark.
She grew up by the first bridge as they built it, you can see in early photos,
black boned skeletons of ox or stag,
the space that hangs between
is breathless air, it reaches out for contact, like our photograph of Catherine
heavy, oval-cut and lead backed, like the colours of the Forth
on cloudy days so different from the Forth reflecting sun
like precious metals, sometimes looking like it has a song to sing
but that was never in its nature,
when the light is low it takes in everything.

2.

drift into a sea of what is possible
what the sea might touch and where
the sea might take me

as a boy I joined the Boy's Brigade
looking for a place I might belong,
I never stayed but still remember

some part of the songs we sung, how:
We have an anchor/that keeps the soul/
steadfast and sure while the billows roll

but the anchor doesn't always hold
the knotted wrack, or bladder wrack,
lies loose and washed up on the shore
the holdfast broken.

3.

there's that film of you backlit and singing
in a bar and everyone who's in there sings
the songs you wrote, the words sung back at you
taking space from source through heart and lungs to mouth

never good at speaking I would swallow down my words
I'd ball them up and feel their weight inside of me
and thought that I was held upon the surface
of a place I'd barely lived in, never had a word for
lived outside of, looking at the sea
until the sea salt settled on my shoes and clothes
until I thought I'd join the sea
until nothing there could hold me
until fireworks filled the air with light that fell
to earth and made the harbour bright.

It's got lots to do with magnets and the pull of the moon

Thift thift thift (said fast with the emphasis on the f and t) said by the heart of the frightened rabbit, when frightened, said with omniaudient ears standing tall and said with hidden ears pinned to the back of the head – where George lingers and aims the barrel. Unaware of its stalked mind, the Scottish winds, bereft of fresh air, gasps petrol fumes between rabbit's panicked lugs, breathed into panicked lungs. Unflushed under fur, the rabbit's coat was grown and worn from heart to skin, keeping the cold out. *Get out of my heart,* the grey hairballs exacerbate the already overworked heart and vomit loud ba-booms ba-booms trying to expel the hair, shed the coat, feel the cold. Feel the moonlight. But the, preternaturally aged, hairs are rooted, too neutral in colour to find colour for furry cheeks, and so the rabbit was warm but un-warmed to warm thoughts. Still the wind tried to chill and it, or George, whistled idly to dis-quiet the landscape and mock the disquiet in the rabbit.

The whistle bounces. Each streetlamp's bulb flickers on with its intangible touch, pinballing gossip of a scared, little bunny and exposing it under harsh scrutiny and light. False light though, for the moon rabbit was still blocked from view, the downward face obscured by verticality. The people's fancified figure in the moon did not have the magnetism of the moon rabbit (and did not pull them like it did the earth rabbit) and so they did not bolt, impassioned, with their long legs to the tops of mountains and trees to leap and reach for the ethereal orb. They stacked blocks, however, *high*, higher than some mountains and some trees. The skyline was littered with ladders to the stars, two, three, four rungs too short, but close with strong hind legs and tall, tall ears. That's where the gossiped bunny would go.

But, for now, the tittle-tattle kindled noise and this vertical place was sparked alive, lit synthetically or not. Footsteps came down now, heavy, and the human heat neared. A gasp. "A rabbit!" said with the animated wonder of a child but slurred in speech. Frightened, the camouflaged motionlessness was uncamouflaged and pushed to motion, instinctively running to the burrow to burrow head, body, and ears. The artificial warrened streets of human husbandry were dedicated to the fostering and raising of crooks, crime, and runaways … and rabbits. The built things, coloured grey through the smoke of the fire but lianas-ly growing up to be enveloped in yellow light, shadowed their cleavage and routed mazes in the human's midst. The bulbs couldn't tattle there, the ladders wouldn't allow it – they know the rabbit's ambitions to climb, to make good use of the ladder's *actual* use.

Nestled in the cleft, strategy succumbed to sleep, the only thing to slow a frightened rabbit's heart. A rustle. [thift, thift, thift]. Eyes as large as saucers and speckled like craters of the moon sought the noise despite ears already knowing. The beggar tips his hat.

Leaving the burrow, black-eyed susan's eyeless black watching had watched, the gloved foxes fingering purple-y grabbed back the stubborn rabbit, back to flora and fauna, despite their role as repelers of rodents and lagomorpha. The nest yelled:

"The beggar will not come to you. If the beggar does come to you, you will not give a great enough sacrifice. You will not jump into the fire. You will be outfoxed. You will be out-monkeyed. You will not become a moon rabbit. You will not! You will not! You will not!"

Chanted as if rehearsed. Frightened by nature, frightened rabbits frighten our frightened rabbit, but our frightened rabbit pressed on. The grass is greener there but the moon is green cheese.

Now on grassless ground, the rabbit within growled at the rabbit outwith as hunger stirred and the beggar within growled at the beggar outwith. The rabbit had nothing to give, no grass, and no fire to throw oneself on. The beggar did not ask for grass or for burning flesh. In fact, the beggar didn't beg. The beggar instead grunted, and the rabbit articulated eloquently its love for the moon:
"How old is the moon? A very old soul. A very good soul. A very old and good soul. I am in love with the moon. To me, the moon is a good reason to grow old. I was made by and for the moon. I long for the cold and the weightlessness, I have craters in my eyes, poking my irises, and a silver crescent sheened coat. My life: it's got lots to do with magnets and the pull of the moon. [translated from rabblish]." The non-begging beggar begs an ajar door open with his tattered right boot and, again, tips his hat.

Probably, a whispered thanks uttered betwixt whiskers, forgotten but genuine. Leaping hind legs exerted clambering up, not rungs but steep steps with impatient haste. Thift, thift, thift, (quiet heart, you are not frightened). The gravitational non-gravitational pull to the sky ensnares and bounces the rabbit up buoyantly, lightens the body mass, levels the flight. The moon *wants* the rabbit as much as the rabbit wants the moon. Three more leaps and the door atop the stair is ajar, left opened with the left beggar's left shoe, and the moon is the entire world. In the middle of the moon, the frightened rabbit doesn't feel so frightened, actually doesn't feel fucking frightened at all. No jittering, shaking, flitting, agitating, shaking, twitching, or quivering. For a moment, in the middle of the moon there was stillness. Then, the leap, a gift between lovers. Thanks were advanced to the Scottish wind for carrying the serene rabbit home. Across the sky, amidst stars, strong hind legs and tall, tall ears closed the gap from the reaching ladder to the moon.

Get into my heart.

Shed your coats and submerge in comfort. Unfrightened, peaceful rabbits. Burrowing in craters, grazing on green cheese, uncamouflaged by moonlight, but not afraid.

This is a story but you're not in it

I wonder whether the pleasure of making
a daisy-chain would be worth the trouble of getting

up and picking the daisies. My head is dead,
unwell. Oh dear! Oh dear! I shall be late.

I'm a frightened rabbit. It's hard to be an artist
when you wobble, clench and shatter.

Read the creed that there is no one like you.
Get out of the bed and pick the daisies.

Down, down, down. Will the fall *never*
come to an end? Here's the Queen—the Red

One who shouts *Off with his head! Off*—
& she sets you free.

Bereft of all Social Charms

The first time I heard The Woodpile, I longed to be a poet. The song not only sounded like a dream, it felt like one too. On a train from Dublin to Kerry (a three-hour journey), I listened to The Woodpile. Over and over, hearing something different in each listen. A poet could surely name what I was feeling, this ethereal trance that was both familiar and terrifying.

Terrifying, because I felt as if I had been seen; as if my carefully hidden loneliness had had the covers ripped off it, like a child hiding in bed, scared of the monsters. How was it, I wondered, that a man I had never known, a man lost to so many, could summon the ache I had lived with for years.

Sad eyed girls and surly boys love to say they are lonely; they love to feign that pain; pouty and delicate in their imagined distress, hinting at it on social media. They adore the idea of glamourous torture, the delicious indulgence of nobody understanding how alone you are. I've always felt that only the very beautiful people can indulge in that kind of behaviour. If you are the kind of woman who has made her romantic life rich with haunting looks and sepia tinted kisses, then these words, my words, are not for you. If you are the sharp boned boy, with even sharper words, who sang of his love of the alternative (but that alternative was for beauties in velvet), these words are not for you, either. I thought to be lonely you had to be alone.

Actually, as a teenager I probably (definitely) romanticised the notion of being lonely. Box black hair held back with gaudy skull clips, self-loathing in a body too big for me and listening to a solid diet of My Chemical Romance, I was actually very happy. Pain, real pain, had not touched me yet. Oh I hated college, hated my looks, hated that I did not have a boyfriend. But I still did not understand that loneliness isn't just to do with being single.

Loneliness is a room you have to sit in, the air heavy with the knowledge that you cannot get out. This room has a window, all the better to see your past mistakes and current demons running around outside, holding hands and smirking in at you.

Loneliness is being with a man who makes you feel as if you're locked in that room.

Loneliness is knowing that the mistakes you have made are yours alone, and nobody will ever be able to share them with you. Loneliness is not just about being alone. Loneliness is a mirror held up to you.

Loneliness is being on holiday with your boyfriend and smelling your mother's perfume; it is your friend walking ahead of you and not hearing you call them; it is the place you go where it is just you, and you alone, and you have no alternative but to look your choices in the eye. Loneliness is when you realise you are an adult, that loss of innocence when you become aware that every mistake you make, no matter how small, will always own you in some way.

Loneliness is allowing cruel people to mock you and deride you and laughing along, betraying yourself and having to meet your eyes in the mirror later, sad and sick about the lies you let them believe about you, about the lies you helped them create.

Loneliness is sitting in a very cold McDonalds at 2am and catching sight of your sad, tired face, make-up streaked and your hair a mess, seeing the story you painted on sliding away.

Loneliness is when you've spent too long alone (tonight).

Although there are so many varied ways to be lonely and it doesn't just have to do (to my mind, anyway) with human contact, I must say that I think Scott Hutchison is beseeching someone he yearns for madly to join him, in The Woodpile.

I was certain I could write this piece and not stoop to mentioning my own feelings of unrequited love, but here we are.

Maybe loneliness isn't the absence of a human, of a partner, but of a feeling; of knowing there is nobody out there who is thinking of you, who is checking their phone one last time before they go to bed in the hopes you might message them. It's the knowledge that there is nobody in the world burning for you, overwhelmed by you, and you alone. It is the taxi ride home, when you've finally waved your friend and her partner away, insisting they go on home. It's another kind friend urging her boyfriend to buy you a drink, like you are the spinster aunt at a wedding reception. I've never been able to decide if it is worse to have absolutely zero romantic prospects, or to love someone who you simply don't exist to.

Anger and loneliness form an unexpected friendship, a duo that drives your fury from the drums and barking, before leaving you exhausted and desperate to escape the collapsing building.

It is the sheer frustration, of being an adult, not a gauche teenager, but an adult woman who knows her own mind and wanting to shake that person, the person who just can't break down the door, much as you want them to.

It's when the wine stops tasting sweet and turns bitter in your mouth. That crushing moment when your keep your brightest smile in place when you go to the bathroom, make-up cracking under the bright, harsh lights..when you look at the carefully painted face and realise all of your makeup, all of your humour (oh, always the humour.."You're the funniest girl I know"..) and your fabulous taste in music didn't fool him, it failed to weave a magic spell around him and all you have left..is your sadness. It's wishing you could torch the entire woodpile, instead of very, very carefully dabbing away the tears before you go back to feign interest in the girl he actually wants..she's never that friendly, you've never heard her make anyone laugh, but God, she's pretty.

Maybe that's why The Woodpile gets to me so much; the words evoke that breath catching feeling, that crush of air, when you are so tired and you just want to tell the person you love to come and find you, to speak in your language, to absolve your loneliness. It's simply wanting your person to be in your corner. Won't they come and break down that door?

Loneliness is finding someone who you think can speak in secret tongues with you, only to find they don't know your language after all.

I have had dark days where I have managed to keep my dignity; where I have laughed off my pain and belittled it. I have covered it, put it to bed, tried to soothe it. Then there are some mornings, sitting on a packed bus, or walking around town by myself when the shops are closing and it's getting dark, when the pain jumps out at me, the real monster in the dark, tearing off the covers.

Loneliness is that tiny speck of hope you hold on to, the edge of pleading in your tone; it's Scott Hutchison imploring you to "come find me now".

I think that's why I keep listening to The Woodpile. The song has a lot of different layers; it is an ode to loneliness in so many ways, and of the frustration and anger that comes from that. It is the sad acceptance of being bereft of all social charms. It is wanting to get out of a room that is mirrored with your own sadness and past mistakes, the mistakes you have been making for years. It is frustration, dark and ripe.

And yet, it is hope.

When Scott Hutchison implores his person to come and find him, to brighten his corner, to speak in a secret tongue..well, I can't help but feel, at the very end of the song, after each listen, that Scott's intended did break down the door, eventually. Because maybe asking for the same thing repeatedly isn't always pathetic; maybe it's knowing that there is someone who will listen, who will come and find you, who will help you light the woodpile and shed light on all of your dark corners.

You just have to find the person who's going to hand you that torch.

The Apprehension of This Eloquence

Explosions always aim for the eye
and sharpness aims for the throat.
The only sensation I feel amongst
the empty inside. Although this
is void of brevity, the gospel
spills a word of clarity and the foolish
will heed every syllable
because we're no good at
building in a room with no floors.

I Still Hear You in the Distance

We hoped you would dream forever
but I worried death sat on your lip.
It would be easier to have never met you
than sit here in pain thinking about
how you've fucked everything up.
My belly called your name
when they said to trust my gut;
I'm clinging to memories like a Henley
in the rain and I feel my heart
is so visibly shaken, that I do my best
to button up. Standing between animosity
and concern—I'm saying words I don't mean
as they drift like a body downstream.
The rain hits the moving water
but there's no distinction just as these
thoughts resting on my head
because you're gone now.
None of it makes a difference.

Glasgae Blessin'

I feel loss
lit a missin' body part
or organ
liver shrivelled
intae nuthin'

Grief is the sea lappin'
it ma feet
But the water is also
lit peace
mouldin' thae sand granules
Intae glass
solid, steady
suttin' thit can withstand
a testament tae cold wind legacy
Whit a shame a live in the city

Step oot the close
god, thit rain feels gid oan ma skin
Scratching, tearing
take a bite oot o' me

I feel lit kindness only comes
fae gritted teeth

In days where pubs remind me
Whit shelter feels lit
Where a shaking haund holding a lighter
Both protected enough tae ignite
I greet intae blue smoke
because I prefer the sound o'rain
on yer skin
instead of oan oak

Cold wind legacy
braces me fir words I'll choke
oan first

"a stiff drink in the pub will set yae right" you say

"anchor yae tae the groon' when gravity fails yae" he says

A breath o' a blessin;

may red sandstone tenements
bear the weight of yae
in yer time o'need
an offer o' a Glasgae kiss
but no the kind you mean
it might no leave you bleedin'
but gie it a try
this time wae feelin'.

The Old Hairdressers

Steam rose
from our breath and laughter
bloomed in open bar doors
that let the night
kiss
and tangle with
us
like the old days.
I think of reaching out for her hand,
spinning her soft self into my arms
in that old, old fashioned way.

"Should have rolled that inside"
I can't quite hear her over
the band
from inside.
"Should have rolled that inside!"
she says a bit louder
as I crouch behind her,
winter cauld
biting my fingers
as I try and hold this wee snout
together.

The street grumbles beneath us,
littered with cigarette butts,
stolen pint glasses
and stumbling folk
that only drink at this time of year
falling on their arses,
outside the old hairdressers.
It's no even midnight yet.

"Where we going after this?"
she asks
"My pal's band haven't played yet"
I exhale blue smoke
accidentally into a passer by's face
he glares,
"aye cheers hen"
I think of snarling, showing my teeth like a dog
I can't remember why I was so angry back then.

Odd socks

With love to 'The Midnight Organ Fight'

All our dead friends came for dinner
and ate until their clothes were freckled with spaghetti.
He poured the final bottle of wine with slurred ceremony,
and said he'd like to die by laughing himself to death.
Said there's articles online - a Greek painter, a dog trainer, some Roman bloke -
who laughed so hard at a joke they died.
I coaxed him, *enough.*
An uncertain blush dappled their dead cheeks, air stained by hush, but
drunk deaf to unseeing he doubled down, and swore he'd laugh in death's
face til he cried.
Excuses were made. Our friends slipped outside to fade away.
I swept the plates and double-locked the door
while he checked all the mirrors in the house to reassure – yes, still invisible -
and then slept snoring on the floor of my room.
 Fumes of his burnt toast woke me. He'd dreamt he'd turned the corner of
Orion's Belt,
unseen by all humanity,
and finally felt that he could breathe and be himself.
We drank right through that feverish year,
chasing the scuffed seam between sea and sky,
a match in his teeth to strike
against the tinder crease of the low light.
Each final voyage to the liquid surge
we came out colder and bluer than reptile blood.
He said it was in his nature. That the urge for the bar is like a sick dog
drawn to the depths of the garden
because you only drink like this if you're cursed.
We headlocked each other in the clutch of a modern Madonna
and sang a damn fine love song into a sonnet.
He was breathless with whispers at each homecoming, warned
that these villages trapped in the saddest of shires
housed a murder of liars. Built to keep war memorials admired and newly
engraved with names
pressganged from the same pebble-dashed estates, where
kicked-shin kids were told to stop fighting gravity

and died on first contact with reality.

Museum homes where mams let us divide unsaved video games
stacked in a box by the base of the bed where the last folded wash
was short of one sock – a pair split. One had kicked hard,
locked in a spin cycle, keeping head above water,
and the other stayed filthy, dropped in the forgot-your-kit box,
tattooed with slide-tackles from the unfinished kick-off.
Dead friends in odd socks – every dinner this
gang knocks with their dressing gown cords spooled into floral bouquets,
clutching boxed salads of mixed bathroom cabinet loot.
We promise each time to meet again soon.
This suit has been hoisted on the hanger for so long
it's the only reason I'm stood up at all.
I called God, but it went straight to voicemail
so left a message and told him He'd failed.
That I'd given up my most trusting years and fuck knows I tried but now my
home is playing host
to Fatherless sons made lonely ghosts
and every time I'd prayed in my room and told out my soul
the silence poured in like a flood.
All we hear is the howl of a wolf who cried boy in the absence of faith
and the laughter of friends who pile up their plate
and are flecked by the marks that Bolognese makes.
Our last suppers aren't laid to prove that we're holy
or that laughing yourself to death isn't a choice to console me,
only that odd socks rolled together seem a little less lonely.

A Little Lick of Paint

By the ledge
or is it knowledge?
He painted as a Virgo.
Maybe to see better the claustrophobic symphonic skys
Yes, I said skys - always plurals.

The edge below us is zion
mine and yours, a treacherous whine.
Between precious bootleggers,
a genius was never born.

The absolute muck of it all,
a storm disguised through zeugma
      - is the use of a verb with two or more complements,
      - playing on the verb's polysemy for humorous effect
but you were laughing already…

Might the fulminous rumble
of sugar beat moons, in a hysteria
porter on the logical fallacy
of using music as a true premise -
A proposition that is yet to be proved;
bred and born being a reversal of normal order.
"I know you're listening
I know you're there."

I'm the Shit and I'm Knee Deep in it

I'm working on this backwards walk counting stars and both those moons.

I'm working on these moods, this mourning, all these stops and starts, chaos.

I've been working on my walking wrong at breakneck speeds forth into fords.

I've been working on my blindness and my blindness and my brain.

I'm working on intrusive thoughts and the drugs and crying and shame.

I'm working on these zero-point dreams that tell me all hands are barometers.

I've been working on small time-sensitive shifts, centre to peripheral to centre.

I've been working on the ocean and the wind and a way to haunt colours.

I've been working on creating planets and letting them set sail.

I'm working on widening ways my end can be called a revelation.

I'm working on a complex sigh four seconds before I hit the ground.

I'm working on real contact highs and I'm working on falling apart.

I'm working on gathering up all of my loose change.

The Mouse

They had been on the rocks for years, but it took Martin until an incidental flicking of the living-room light switch to truly feel it. As the bulb grew to glow, the whimpering he had gone to investigate faltered, a deep breath and a catching throat. Cara's sofa slouching form betrayed the weak smile she attempted to pass off as real. He stepped hesitantly through the doorway, shrinking impossibly small for such a large man.

A despondent call and response of 'hey' was aired out in awkwardness.

Cara held out cupped hands to exhibit a small sock, balled up in itself. She was weeping again. Stepping further into the room, Martin's poor sight was aided by proximity: the sock his wife was displaying was not in fact a sock but a dead mouse; and their ageing tabby, Bertie, was sprawled over her feet, looking charmingly smug.

Cara glanced down at their proud pet. The glance, Martin observed, was full of love in a way that hadn't been true to a single look she'd given him in years. He dropped his eyes to the cat, intending to glare a spike of jealousy at him, but Bertie was too sweet and so this look also turned to love. Cara gulped as she saw the same thing in Martin's glance at Bertie as he had seen in hers.

Momentarily he tried to kid himself that she was upset for the life of the mouse she was cradling. In Bertie's kittenhood, each dead mouse prompted a certain sadness in her, without devaluing her love of the cat himself. She had always recognised the affectionate intentions in the gift of a mouse. Those were the days, they thought in tandem, perhaps thinking in the same vein as each other for the first time since then.

His age and increasing immobility had rendered mouse-catching a hobby of the past, it had been years. The lengths Bertie had gone to showing his affection in his own way were evidenced by the raw paws and limp limbs he now rested at Cara's feet. She had neither given nor received such a gesture in a long time. The mouse was beautiful, she thought, and so was Bertie and his lifetime of kindness.

The couple locked eyes, and Cara cried thinking of their funny cat and laughed thinking of their sorely lost love. Martin tried to find something similar within himself, but could not. He switched the light back off.

I am in a long-distance relationship

with the past. Film strip
      for bookmarks. Circa love era,

a torch only serves
      to make the darkness brighter.

Yet, somehow, still smaller
      in a room with the lights turned off?

      Forever saluting
the lonely crow

      in a field full of magpies.

10/05/18

The mourners check the news on their phone. The mourners don't take their headphones out. The mourners sit on their swivel chair. The mourners have nothing to do. The mourners look at rivers. The mourners look at rivers. The mourners look at rivers. The mourners shuffle their feet in conference halls. The mourners eat veggie ham sandwiches. The mourners spend £5.80 on ale. The mourners don't talk in lifts. The mourners don't check the time. The mourners look at rivers. The mourners have fillings. The mourners run knuckles across radiators. The mourners look for themselves in everything. The mourners look at rivers. The mourners can't sing. The mourners can't write. The mourners look at rivers, get tattoos, look at rivers, look at rivers.

Kingfisher

Grief needs time to filter through
is this a poem about him, me or you?

Memory takes variable Polaroids
some fade while others accrue:

Just as you were breaking
my pink iPod drew Sanquhar schoolroom curiosity

'Look, Jules likes Frightened Rabbit.'
'Yeah, they live in Selkirk too.' 'Cool.'

Told them my kids saw you at T in the Park
then sneaked you on my retro playlist

among their Goth, Emo and Indie stuff.
Check out *Sing the Greys* discography

Hutchison a different kind of libertine to Doherty.
The white titles would still rest in black

if the device wasn't obsolete, hairline cracked.

                    ****

Talking to Billy's proud Dad Larry on the Selkirk street
trying to sound casual, not too excited or indiscreet

how you were making another album, maybes touring the States
success creates its own snowball traction

highs and lows need to be kept in perspective.
And then the disappearance, your face on Reporting Scotland

believe, hope, anyone can have a 'lost weekend'
even in three bridge South Queensferry.

But when I see Larry, he is totally numbed
I think I saw bandmembers outside Sir Walter's Courtroom

that blank expression 'what do we do now?'
Unspoken: 'Who can possibly write those songs?'

****

Selkirk Graveyard is a local Père Lachaise
I'm with a girl looking for her Aunt on the stones

I wonder if she remembers? Memory plays tricks
are hers selective, not wishing to be recalled?

We become aware of kids lurking, furtive at the top
speculate they are fans looking, mourning for Scott

a lime line between worship and respect
friends and family exist beyond whinstone monoliths

who don't seek to be morbid, Byronically depressed.
But living in Selkirk can entail feeling different

to a sly unyielding machismo culture
you turn in on yourself to reach a sense of belonging

to gain universal Border outsiderdom
found in poetry, music, love and painting.

****

Down by Ettrick River the shy kingfisher sings
bright blue in the tree of loneliness and despair

on a shrine, on posts in the Haining
'make tiny changes' the message still sticks

moving into the future it's what we all must do
not merely mouth easy box tick platitudes.

Like a song, a poem is the heart's true construction.
Today Forget Me Nots and May blossom slowly peep through

is this more a poem about them, her, me or you?

Ramshackle

The shelter is holey, teetering
On small flats of grass, rusty troughs buttress one side.
It noticeably leans. The hillside of old skins
The flock yearly. You're here to see
If you can work remotely, and sure enough. There
Is the sound of paper tearing far away.
That circus places rocks on your door, and hence here
With the suggestion of people
Long ago. Maybe this is how it'll all end.
You, without foreshadow, ascend this peak and find
Stones supporting stones, no roof, and incredible aloof sheep.
Let's hide here a while. Here
Where you can't see or hear the water.

Critical feedback

My grandad was not a poem
Until he died
He was three minutes and nine seconds long so
I cut him back

And the grief became softer in the sun

Home Videos
after Poke

You should look through some old photos

Your baby face is mottled with raspberry acne but your eyes haven't grown
their violet under circles yet, despite you drinking more cherry cola than
water. He has inherited his grandad's car and recently peeled the learner
plate away, his teeth still pushed into straight confines by metal and wires.
The gap between driver and passenger seat is rose-tinted with hormones and
unspoken things. The two of you are always hatching a plan or gossiping,
bickering over who introduced the other to your favourite band, catching
secret glimpses of each other, low budget coming of age film protagonists.
Both desperate to be hedonistic and interesting but burdened with the same
anxious lump in your throat at parties. Nail biters, best friends, will-they-
won't-they, the intake of breath before a tower-block demolition. Cowering
at the back of the science lab together, retching at the frog dissection. Young,
still just two kids. Tadpoles.

I adored you in every one of those

Most of your time is spent sweating for £3.72 an hour, apron tied so tightly
around your middle that it is training your waist to permanently suck in. A
bowl of hot water rests on the counter to soak the metal scoop in, to make
the ice cream malleable: easier for you to dig into and for your boss to milk
profit from. Tiny biceps are forming beneath your pink polo shirt sleeves. You
pour the cloudy water down the toilet and refill it under the tap twice a day
during busy shifts. At the end of each afternoon, when you have closed the
hatch, wiped the freezer down and peeled your disposable latex gloves off,
you step out into the heaving city, your hamstrings gnawing in protest at the
uphill walk to the train station. Your cheeks glow when you read the string of
messages he has sent to your phone while it's been left in your bag. Your mum
sees how your once soft heels have become cracked and hardened, hands you
a tub of peppermint foot cream like she is passing on a relay race baton, says:
"Prevention is better than cure, but it looks like it's too late for that". Your body will
never be the same again and you don't even pause for breath.

Remember it was me who dragged you up to the sweaty floor

Your weekly minimum wage packets have finally bloomed into something
solid and tangible. You buy festival tickets sitting side by side on his bed,

almost touching. His wallpaper hasn't been redone since he was a baby; circus performers dance above the border, all of them manic and squabbling. At the festival you are crushed together in sticky crowds, showered with beer and piss when a plastic cup is chucked over your heads. The lengths of your hair acquire a fetid and sweet stench. It feels like hours of searching until you find your tent in the wet dark; your voices crispy and hollowed out from hours of screaming lyrics; juicy plum bruises already sprouting beneath jeans and tights. Your bodies slot neatly into the same half zipped sleeping bag. You are dizzy with his David Beckham aftershave, holding in a wee because if you interrupt the moment now, it might be put to one side and forgotten about. The next morning you concoct a cosmopolitan while he goes in search of something hot and greasy to soak up your hangovers. Vodka, orange juice sweet talked from a stoned man in a neighbouring tent, and a cranberry cystitis relief sachet. You think you should work in a fancy cocktail bar and not in an ice cream hut. You spit a mouthful of toothpaste onto the grass then watch it foam, a sterile puddle in the dirt. On the way home, stuck in a traffic jam, your mouths meet in the gap between driver and passenger seat. You don't pull apart until the car horn behind beeps. He sticks a middle finger up at them out of the window — tries to drive on, but stalls. You shrink down into your seat.

We adopt brand new language

There is a fresh shyness festering beneath the surface as if you haven't known each other for years already. A new baby bud forming from an adolescent stem. You feel like a whole adult at the cash point, taking a ten pound note out before meeting him at the pub, where you still have to hide in a booth at the back while he gets served for you both. Just on the cusp of old enough. You are all lace push-up bra and eyeliner wings. Too giddy to fall asleep some nights, wriggling limbs around your side of his single bed in an attempt to wake him up. Spluttering everywhere when you try to show off your smoke rings in the park. A pact to not mention exam results or the other people you got with at parties pre-budding romance. You float through weeks of morning afters, flashing your expired student bus pass when you get the bus home in his trackies and socks.

If you don't want to be with me, just say and I will go

You are independent now, away from home, a grown up. But not eating enough. Reaching out for the snooze button in your sleep, waking up late and groggy in the afternoon still wearing yesterday's clothes. Aching to be back with people who know you inside out. He is miles away: blossoming into a social butterfly, tagged in a new Facebook photo every other night, decorated in neon paint or at a foam party, trying new things, leaving you behind. His voice on the phone is a syrup to dilute your homesickness in, but the guilt writhes in your gut when you call too often, knowing he is doing just fine without you. Better.

Why won't our love keel over, as it chokes on a bone

Your housemate complains that the two of you giggling through the wall keeps her up at night when he's visiting. You often wake up sweat soaked from a nightmare where the thin walls are caving in on you until you are buried in layers of tissue paper, suffocating. His visits are sometimes matching costumes at the Student Union club nights, legs tangled under blankets, greedy mouthfuls of a shared wrap from the falafel van. Dopamine, serotonin, oxytocin. But there are also fights. Whole wars. You are always trying to roll the post argument shame back into the sleeping bag compression sack but can't find a way to make it fit again. Once they leave your mouth you find that the words expand and are impossible to flatten. You feel sick with love for him underneath the heady glow of nightclub strobes. You are sure that one day you will tell your children not to do the reckless things you do together; you are sure there will be children who are half him, half you.

And now we're unrelated, and rid of all the shit we hated

Your housemates will sleep better now. When he has closed the door of your student house for the last time; connected lock with latch, driven away in his grandad's car, not changed his mind and turned back; you sit halfway up the stairs like a child waiting for someone to come home and put you to bed. Hours pass before you move. You listen to the dripping tap. He didn't wind it tight enough before leaving. You call your oldest friend for the first time in months, the smashed glass of your phone screen tiny rivulets with bursting flood banks, explain in ugly gulps that he has washed his hands of you. Somebody calls your dad. Maybe it was you. He drives for miles through the night to come and collect you and take you home. He leaves the child lock on like he always does, a force of protective habit. You howl into your knees; wish you had left things alone. It feels like the pain could knock you out with one swift blow, and you would welcome the relief.

But I hate when I feel like this, and I never hated you

Everything is unfurling. You mostly sleep and run up your parents' gas bill with endless hot baths. It feels safer to sob in water. You stay in the nest, only venturing out to take bags of his clothes to charity shops. Skulking home to watch his handwriting ribbon through the teeth of the shredder, eat instant noodles, leave voicemails, send streams of hysterical texts. Flittering between all five stages of grief. Your mum comes home from work one night and you curl up on the sofa together in your dressing gowns, watching old home videos on the TV. All of your flaws yet to blossom. Chubby hands pulling two halves of a plastic watermelon apart. A play tent with a hatch to serve imaginary ice creams from. Eating cherries on the back step with your brother, spitting the stones at each other. You understand it's time to leave the nest again now. You go back. You begin to claw advice from every stranger you meet in club smoking areas, desperate to be fixed and neatly repaired so you can be sent back out into the world new and glittering. You try lying awake in the unfamiliar smell of strangers' bedsheets and hate it. When you are with new friends who have never known him, or you when you were part of him, you sometimes catch a laugh escaping your mouth, and don't clamp your lips together in time to trap it. Sometimes you set an alarm to watch the sun come up by the harbour and decide to walk the scenic route home afterwards.

If someone took a picture of us now, they'd need to be told that we had ever clung on tight

You have found a third-year house with a bath. A cobwebbed one admittedly, with spiders you had to coax out onto your palm and rehome in the safe space beneath the sofa. You are sitting on the porcelain edge, sleepy and soft bodied, working peppermint foot cream into your heels. You only notice the song come on through the speakers because your shoulders stiffen on reflex. His voice still lingers beneath the harmonies. You remember how he used to belt the chorus, windows down, thumbs drumming on the steering wheel. But the urge to skip onto the next song is gentler than it once was; no longer visceral and choking, now just a toddler nervously tugging on your sleeve. You allow your nose to twitch, and the salty tears to prick your eyes until they spill over. You hope he has just got out of a hot bath, too. You hope he is looking after himself, taking multivitamins, getting enough sleep. You hope you never bump into each other on a night out or in the post office queue, that your paths have crossed for the last time. Later, you notice yourself humming the same song, the one you have avoided for all this time, that the notes sound almost whole again between your teeth.

Keep Warm

In our porridge era
 heartsore by the open door
  of the early daze
 tenement loneliness
  stupid acoustic caress
we
  disintegrate

at the cost of living
eleven lives ago
 already too late
      crescenting
  in the scifi sky
playing our favourite lament
so fast
 at the afters
  played it to death
 in the freezing bedroom
shouting for nourishment
in the arms of one-syllable boys
 swapping callouses for
  each tang of fingered steel
   deep in no time
  being teenage
       in house beats

 the difference is
  whether you can show your wounds
   or sugar them

    metallurgy of regrets

but I love the fucked past
 sucking frostbitten thorns
  losing my new hair barrette and pills on the bus

every cool lustre like a joke
 lying intensely awake
in the look of you
   clearing your throat at the end of all things
          flying by the Clyde
        still brightness
        lowering brightness
just being us
 wanting to touch each other, to never go
   totally home
singing
 you are so calm
 you are long in the world
   and goldenhoured
      come down from there.

Low Ceilings

Afraid of the warm tides of history.
A stairful of wilting penstemons
pressing up against your neck
instead of a coherent ideology.
My love for you tending to ward
against building novel theories or
scraped like a heart against low
expectations & concrete pleasures.
We told all of your static and voice
mails only for them not to listen.
Just a darkening. Let's not waste love
on more lonesome collaborations.

OCEAN WRESTLE

They tore me limb from limb
There is bone, there is gristle
I'm despairing
— Scott Hutchinson

dark waters plunge into her
arm meets only air the boat
far beyond the horizon now
she supposes
shadow shapes blend below
ghoulish diver rises in greeting
his feral figure
resembles her own
both animals are clotheless
sea demon grins
as if this a fair fight makes
tail tremble; let's play
slow-move fight
her dearth of inhalations
gilled creature, foot-in-maw
down again they go
her un-drown ability
does not serve her
though she will float face-up
endebted to yellow
sharp teeth never pierce skin
her unmauled limbs
do not leave behind
a diluted rust-red trail

Promises

It's a glorious January day, the sun casting a nostalgic glow over post-industrial central Scotland. Dad pulls two brollies out the boot.

'Ah you never know do you,' is the Calvinist response when I hesitate.

We negotiate the creaky old turnstiles and listen to the pre-match buzz, as familiar supporters reacquaint themselves with one another.

An old lad is trying to listen to the radio updates through his phone. He turns to a boy, a quarter of his age, to ask him to fix the volume because he couldn't manage the wee buttons or the wee screen.

'Never hud any a this bother wae the aul wireless.'

The young lad obliges, presumably no idea what a wireless is.

They all settle themselves into position.

Over the damaged roof of the single stand, rusted from years of perpetual storms, the Ochils, resplendent against their clear blue background. Long and undulating, uncertain peaks, shades of earthy green and dull browns jigsawing up the gradual climbs, shadows wandering aimlessly along. Hills I could see from my childhood bedroom window, seen in a new light. Almost worth the entry fee.

My nose draws me to the pie stand; hot vinegar and pastry. The half-time pie and bovril is served with forcefulness. The pie is crispy on the thin crust and soft everywhere else, the meat inside congealed into a single entity. Brown sauce covers the pie as if it had no other place to be. The Bovril is gritty, salty and hotter than the sun, the polystyrene cup doing nothing to protect my numbing fingers.

After the game, I wondered about asking Dad if he fancied a pint, but I knew what the answer would be.

'Och, I'd love to, but best get home to your Mum. Not nice to leave her alone for too long.'

She was always his priority. Is always.

>   *Let's promise every girl we marry*
>   *We'll always love them*
The next line is
>   *when we probably won't*

but, as we drive home on familiar back roads with equally familiar voices summarising the day's football on the radio, I glance at my dad, both hands on the steering wheel at ten to two, and I think about what I could be, and what love can be.

Crawling

I'm singing the greys for you while the sea bleeds. I wish I could have danced in a communal heart, been your *Catcher in the Rye*. But I missed my chance to hide the matches, to build a fence across the shore, to hide the rusted spade and rope, to fill in all the holes. So I'm singing the greys for you, for those who weren't saved by a boat or a blue flash in the road. My sister could have been you but was saved. I could have been you but was saved. There are millions of us that can't resist, won't come round again. I'll be singing the greys again while lightning crackles in my brain, still singing, still swimming on through these damned old greys.

The best bits are coloured in

Most of us is water not yet to evaporate.
Another part is metal   real in its own way.
I suppose I'm trying to tell you
not to underestimate the moon.

I washed our fossil in the upstairs sink.
Its dust predates us here,
and if we're doing this,
some things are going to break.
Only we have stuff that won't be snapped
unlike that mouse in the jaws of that cat.
Where there's love in dogeared photographs
it will for always be.

I am saved by you.

Laura Theis' work appears in *Poetry, Mslexia, Rattle, Asimov's,* etc. Her poetry debut 'how to extricate yourself', an Oxford Poetry Library Book-of-the-Month, won the Brian Dempsey Memorial Prize. Her music is available on Bandcamp and was featured on *Welcome to Night Vale.*

Ian Farnes is a writer and translator from Fife, who grew up by the Firth of Forth. More information is available at his website: Ianfarnes.com. He would like to thank the artist Clare Archibald for her help.

Emma Whitelaw is an English Literature UoG MA graduate and Napier undergraduate in English and Film. She is published in Glasgow zines, including *Dolls zine, CHEWGULPSPIT, morii,* and *Queer Futures.* Emma's favourite theme when writing is magic in mundanity.

Alice-Catherine Jennings lives in Santa Fe, New Mexico. Her newest book of poetry is *Quilling Will* (Assure Press, 2021).

Caitriona Murphy lives in Dublin with her family and familiars. She has had over sixteen stories published, online and in print, and is working on her first novel. Catriona adores words, music and the moon.

Anthony Desmond is the author of *Martyrs of a Certain Belief* (Thirty West Publishing House, 2020). Desmond's poetry is honest, unadulterated and breaches the norms of the expected—bold statement pieces that are granular observations of the world.

M McCorquodale is a working class, Glaswegian poet. She has performed at a variety of events across Scotland from punk gigs to poetry events. In print, M has a collection *What I Told Frank* (2018) and a pamphlet *Confession* (2021).

Geraint Ellis is a Welsh Northumbrian poet. He is a Barbican Young Poet and former Scottish National Slam Poetry Finalist. He was shortlisted for the 2022 Aesthetica Creative Writing Prize, 2022 Bridport Prize and 2022 Aurora Prize. His work is published by flipped eye publishing, Abridged and more, and he has written for BBC Radio Comedy.

Michelle Moloney King is a poet, artist, cygnet at Beir Bua Press & Design student. Her work communicates the tension between the living and the dead; as if a warning or hope. www.MichelleMoloneyKing.com

Jo Higgs (he/him) lives in Edinburgh, where he is from and is yet to escape. Recently he won the Sloan Prize and was a runner-up in the John Byrne Award. His story in this anthology is inspired by a lyric in the song 'Poke'

jade king is a dyslexic poet from the UK. She is often told she "looks like a dog person." Her work has been published or is forthcoming in *3:AM Magazine*, *Schlag Magazine* and *Poetry Salzburg Review.*

Carl Burkitt tells tales: short ones, long ones, sad ones, silly ones. He tells them online, behind a mic, in books, and in schools. He's had words published by *Bad Betty Press*, *Pan Macmillan*, *Beir Bua*, and *Acid Bath Publishing.*

Julian Colton has had five collections of poetry published including *Everyman Street* (Smokestack Publishing), *Cold Light of Morning* (Cultured Llama) and *Two Che Guevaras (Scottish Borders Council).* He currently works Front-of-House at Sir Walter Scott's Courtroom in Selkirk.

Andrew Blair is a poet, writer and performer living in Edinburgh. He co-produced the Saboteur-nominated *Poetry as Fuck* podcast with Ross McCleary. His pamphlet *The R-Pattz Facttz 2020* was published by Speculative Books and is largely about Robert Pattinsons.

Charlie Rose Evans is a fiction writer from Birmingham, where she works as a receptionist at a trade union. Since graduating from Falmouth University, Charlie has contributed to *Popshot*, *Potluck Zine* and *'So Long as You Write'* (*Dear Damsels*).

Kyle Lovell is a poet, critic and editor of Fathomsun Press. They are the author of *Each Sharper Complication* (legitimate snack, 2020) and *In the Debt of Love* (And False Fire, 2021).

Vita Sleigh has an interdisciplinary illustration and writing practice circling around thoughts of out- and insides, (non)human creatures, and the sea.

Gavin Baird recently completed an MLitt in Creative Writing at Glasgow Uni, and has had stories and poems published by *Gutter Mag, Epoch Press, Speculative Press* and *Scotland Street Press.* His favourite Frightened Rabbit song is Poke.

Lynn Valentine's debut collection, *Life's Stink and Honey,* was published by Cinnamon Press in 2022, after winning the Cinnamon Literature Award. Her Scots language pamphlet, *A Glimmer o Stars,* was published by Hedgehog Poetry (2021), after winning their dialect competition.

Al Crow works across fiction, creative non-fiction and poetry, exploring the climate emergency and human fragility through these mediums. The poem featured here is inspired by *Poke* from *The Midnight Organ Fight.*

LAY OUT YOUR GREYS

Ingram Content Group UK Ltd.
Milton Keynes UK
UKHW040751240423
420680UK00004B/319

9 781915 760920